CALLING THE UNQUALIFIED

Ignite Your Authority and Fulfil Your God-Given Mandate

ESTHER SAMSON

COPYRIGHT

If you purchased this book without a cover, please be aware that it may have been stolen and reported as "unsold and destroyed" to the publisher. In such cases, neither the author nor the publisher has received any payment for the "stripped book."

Copyright © 2025 by Esther Samson

All rights reserved. No part of this book may be reproduced, stored in a retrieval system, or transmitted in any form—whether electronic, mechanical, photocopying, recording or otherwise—without prior written permission from the publisher, except for brief quotations in reviews.

Scripture References:

Unless otherwise stated, Scriptures are taken from the Holy Bible (KJV, NIRV, and NLT) versions.

Published independently via Kindle Direct Publishing

Edited by: Dorcas Fadele

Cover Design by: Munny Aktery

ISBN: 9798312813852

For inquiries, please send an email to:

estherukaria@yahoo.co.uk

TABLE OF CONTENTS

INTRODUCTION A NOTE TO READERS 1

CHAPTER ONE CHOSEN 4

CHAPTER TWO NOW THE WAR BEGINS: THE STAR WATCHERS 24

CHAPTER THREE THE FIRST AWAKENING: HOW I BECAME DEEPLY AWARE OF GOD'S CALL ON MY LIFE 47

CHAPTER FOUR THE PRODIGAL DAUGHTER 57

CHAPTER FIVE BEYOND THE PULPIT 67

CHAPTER SIX THE TRAINING SEASON 77

CHAPTER SEVEN WELCOME TO A NEW SEASON 93

FINAL REFLECTIONS IGNITE YOUR AUTHORITY AND FULFIL YOUR GOD-GIVEN MANDATE 101

OTHER BOOKS BY THE AUTHOR 104

HOW TO LEAVE A REVIEW 106

AUTHOR'S INFORMATION 107

ABOUT THE BOOK 108

ABOUT THE AUTHOR 110

DEDICATION

This book is dedicated to God Almighty, who gives me the wisdom to write it, and to everyone who has ever felt unworthy of the assignment God has placed in their hands. You are the right person for the job!

ACKNOWLEDGMENTS

I want to express my heartfelt gratitude to my mother, Victoria Emmanuel, for encouraging me to write from the young age of nine. To my son, Great Manaty, whose eagerness to read my next work brings me joy. To my critics, your words push me to improve my writing. To my two brothers, Tunde and Mike, and my dearest Aunty B—you are always in my thoughts.

INTRODUCTION
A NOTE TO READERS

THE CALL OF GOD'S REMNANT ARMY

"You are not called to blend in, but to stand out, shine brightly, and bring the kingdom of God to earth." **- Esther Samson**

The world may try to silence you, but your purpose cannot be dimmed. You were made for such a time as this.

In this season, God is calling His remnant army, and you are among the chosen. Despite facing trials, tribulations, and the storms of life, you have remained steadfast. You have refused to bow to the false gods of this fallen world. You have been set apart, hidden for a reason, and watched over by God. You have been refined and prepared for this very moment.

Now, He is activating His League of the Righteous—strategically placed across nations to carry His light into every area of influence: schools, governments, hospitals, businesses, the military, media, and beyond. You have been positioned with purpose, sent as a vessel of His kingdom to reclaim what darkness has held too long.

The fire within you has been growing stronger. That stirring in your spirit is no accident—it is your divine signal. The time to move is now! Step into your God-given assignment with confidence, knowing He has already equipped you for the journey ahead. Do not fear or hesitate. Follow His voice alone and walk boldly in your calling.

Isaiah 43:1 (NLT) reminds us: *"But now, O Jacob, listen to the Lord who created you. O Israel, the one who formed you says, 'Do not be afraid, for I have ransomed you. I have called you by name; you are mine.'"*

The call to step into your divine purpose is clearer than ever. Ephesians 5:8-9 (NLT) declares: *"For once, you were full of darkness, but now you have light from the Lord. So live as people of light! For this light within you produces only what is good and right and true."*

You are the light of the world, and now is your time to shine!

CHAPTER ONE

CHOSEN

"Being chosen is not about perfection; it is about purpose. God does not call the qualified—He qualifies the called. He chooses people not based on their qualifications but on His divine purpose, grace, and their willingness to be used for His glory." - Esther Samson

ANCHOR SCRIPTURE

"You did not choose me. I chose you. I appointed you to go and produce lasting fruit so that the Father will give you whatever you ask for, using my name." - John 15:16 (NLT)

Have you ever felt like you don't belong, like you are just another face in the crowd, unnoticed and unimportant? What if I told you that before you took your first breath, you were already chosen?

God did not bring you into this world by accident. You were intentionally created and handcrafted for a divine purpose. The fact that you are here is proof that God has a plan for you, no matter what life has thrown your way.

WHAT IT MEANS TO BE CHOSEN

To be chosen means more than just being set apart — it means being empowered, appointed, and equipped for something greater than yourself. Consider these words:

- Chosen – exclusive, singled out
- Set apart – distinguished
- Appointed – set in authority
- Spokesman – a representative
- Masterpiece – a gem created in Christ Jesus for His good works

These words are a reminder that you are not here by chance. You are a prized creation of great value to God. From the beginning, you were part of a grand design, ordained to accomplish a specific purpose — the God-given purpose.

God infused a piece of His divine essence into you, forming you in your mother's womb so that you would shine His light and reflect His immeasurable goodness. You were not sent into this world merely for earthly pleasures but to carry out a higher calling.

WHEN LIFE MAKES YOU FORGET YOU ARE CHOSEN

Perhaps you have forgotten why you are here because of the countless shipwrecks you have encountered. Disappointments, failures, and rejections may have made you question if you truly have a purpose. But remember this: God never left you; He overcame it all for you.

Jesus Himself assured us in John 16:33 (NLT): *"I have told you all this so that you may have peace in me. Here on earth, you will have many trials and sorrows. But take heart, because I have overcome the world."*

If God has overcome the world, then no trial or hardship can erase the fact that you are chosen.

GOD QUALIFIES THE UNQUALIFIED

God wants you to know that He does not choose people based on their qualifications but on His divine purpose, grace, and willingness to be used for His glory. The unqualified are often chosen and made qualified overnight.

Consider these individuals:

- **Paul** – once a persecutor of the church, became one of the greatest apostles.

- **Moses** – a murderer who struggled with low self-esteem, yet God used him to lead an entire nation.

- **King David** – whose lustful desires led him into trouble, but God still called him a man after His heart.

These stories show that God's grace can transform anyone, no matter their past. In the eyes of men, they were unfit, yet in the hands of God, they became history-makers. He picked them at different seasons to fulfil His divine purposes, and through them, He brought great glory and victory to His kingdom.

YOU ARE CHOSEN FOR A REASON

You may not see the full picture yet, but trust this: You are chosen for something greater than yourself. You carry divine potential within you, and when you surrender to God's calling, He will position you where you are meant to be.

No matter where you have been or what you have done, God is not done with you. You are chosen, appointed, and set apart for His glory.

Yahweh is strategic in everything He does, and He never makes mistakes. So why doubt His calling on your life? Take Moses, for example—born under unusual circumstances, adopted as a prince in the

Egyptian palace, and eventually used as a tool to set God's people free.

Despite his stutter, Moses possessed unique leadership qualities that God instilled in him, preparing him for his role as a deliverer. Just like Moses, God chose you from your mother's womb, equipping you with unique talents and assignments that only you can carry out. Through the finished work of His Son, Jesus Christ, He granted you the authority to walk confidently in your assignment.

In Jeremiah 1:5 (NLT), God assures you, *"I knew you before I formed you in your mother's womb. Before you were born, I set you apart and appointed you as my prophet to the nations."* This means that even before you took your first breath, God had a plan for you, a specific calling and purpose that no one else could fulfil.

Ephesians 2:10 (NLT) reinforces this truth: "For we are God's masterpiece. He has created us anew in Christ

Jesus, so we can do the good things He planned for us long ago." You are not just an afterthought; you are His masterpiece, uniquely crafted to fulfil His divine purpose.

And, as Psalm 145:9 (NLT) reminds us, *"The LORD is good to everyone. He showers compassion on all His creation."* God's goodness and compassion extend to you, and His calling on your life is a demonstration of that love and care. He will never call you to something without equipping you for it.

LET'S GO BACK IN TIME

I was only nine years old when I began discovering my gifts—writing, singing, a creative mind that birthed solutions, a love for the Gospel, the prophetic, and more. One evening, my mother promised my brother and me that we would spend the weekend playing tennis at Kano Club and enjoy some delicious suya, a routine we had grown fond of.

Just before we left, I closed my eyes for a moment, and a vision flashed before me. I saw a street with a tree crashing down onto our car. My heart raced with fear, and I immediately urged my mother to take a different route to the club. Thankfully, she agreed. When we were driving back from Kano Club that evening, we saw a fallen tree blocking the road. My mother turned to me in shock, both of us at a loss for words, or perhaps even dumbfounded, by what had just happened.

The year passed, and by the time I turned ten and a half, I became increasingly captivated by the things of God, especially whenever visitors came to our home for fellowship. I remember one instance when a woman asked me to pray over her business. As I looked at her, I found myself suggesting that she invest in another company, and then I prayed for her.

The adults around me laughed, likely thinking I was just a child who did not know any better. A few weeks later, she came back to tell my mother that she had followed my advice, and her profits doubled. My mother still could not understand what was happening to me, but she would say, "The Lord told me you were special."

One Sunday, I listened to the bishop's sermon at New Generation Bible Church in Kano. When it was time for the altar call, a force drew me forward. I reached out and tugged at the bishop's suit. With a warm smile, he lifted me up and handed me the microphone.

To everyone's surprise, I declared, "I want to give my life to Christ." My mother rushed forward in disbelief, unsure what had come over her little girl. That incident marked a turning point, leading to a spiritual battle between the devil and light over my life.

As we move on to the next set of insights, I encourage you to take a moment to reflect on every area of your life and begin closing any negative open doors.

CLOSING NEGATIVE DOORS

I declare, "Let there be light in all areas of your life, in Jesus' name." The light of God reveals to redeem, guiding you on what to pray for. John 1:5 (NLT) says, *"The light shines in the darkness, and the darkness can never extinguish it."* This light is not just a symbol—it is the power that reveals and breaks any darkness in your life, allowing God's truth to guide you in prayer and transformation.

Negative open doors include issues such as unforgiveness, strongholds, negative family covenants, the effects of divorce, recurring setbacks, a captive mind that leads to stagnation, self-sabotaging behaviours, lingering trauma, or the impact of past experiences that result in insecurity, unresolved pain, addiction, and more. If they are left unaddressed, they remain open channels for the enemy to operate in your life, hindering your prayers and progress.

If your soul is held captive by the devil, you cannot execute your assignment with success. You must first renounce the strongholds in the name of Jesus Christ, with the help of the Holy Spirit, and by faith. Only then can you begin to walk in freedom, activating the Word of God through constant fellowship with Him. As the Bible reminds us, *"But if we confess our sins to Him, He is faithful and just to forgive us our sins and to cleanse us from all wickedness."* (1 John 1:9, NLT). This forgiveness and cleansing empower you to move forward in God's plan for your life.

My hope is that you will come to truly discover who God created you to be and approach Him with humility and fierce determination as you make these declarations. Remember, it is not by your strength that you can overcome but by the Spirit of the Lord who makes the impossible possible. Only He can restore the years the locusts have stolen, guide you on the right path, and equip you with all you need to be His true fishers of men in the global sectors and various communities.

As you declare His Word, know that *"The heavens declare the glory of God; the skies proclaim the work of His hands. Day after day they pour forth speech; night after night they reveal knowledge."* (Psalm 19:1-2, NIV). Just as God's creation speaks of His greatness, your words, aligned with His truth, carry the power to shape your destiny.

Your words have the power to bring things into being or wreck them. Just as the Word of God is powerful, your words are also powerful. So, words are not something to be taken lightly. You must always declare positively into your situations, using God's Word to break free from any satanic bondage. Everything that unfolds in heaven and on earth has been declared spiritually before it manifests physically. The words of God are filled with life, representing the truth. They are a double-edged sword, cutting through old patterns and breaking generational cycles.

Hebrews 4:12 (NLT) says, *"For the word of God is alive and powerful. It is sharper than the sharpest two-edged sword, cutting between soul and spirit, between joint and marrow. It exposes our innermost thoughts and desires."* The sword is sharpened on both sides, so it can cut through easily. Likewise, the Word of God can cut through any stronghold, but you must first believe and be in a right relationship with God.

The Word of God expresses Jesus Christ through the help of the Holy Spirit.

Therefore, continue to declare your intentions until you witness the new reality you desire—a life of abundance, living in the finished works of Christ, and life as a true son or daughter of God—while you occupy the earth until His return. Remember, as Matthew 6:33-34 (NIRV) encourages us, *"But put God's kingdom first. Do what He wants you to do. Then all those things will also be given to you. So don't worry about tomorrow. Tomorrow will worry about itself. Each day has enough trouble of its own."* Trust that as you focus on God's kingdom and His will, everything else will fall into place.

DECLARATIONS

1. Heavenly Father, I repent for straying from Your path and following my will. I receive Your grace to

seek Your Kingdom daily and walk in Your righteousness. Everything I do— (state it here)— will reflect Your Kingdom on earth and bring glory to Your name, in Jesus' name.

1 Peter 2:9 (KJV): "But you are a chosen generation, a royal priesthood, a holy nation, His own special people, that you may proclaim the praises of Him who called you out of darkness into His marvellous light."

2. Father, I receive Your mercy to become who You have called me to be. I have accepted Jesus Christ, who has freed me from darkness; therefore, I shine as a light to my generation. Old habits of pride, inherited anger, envy, demonic influences, and negative covenants no longer have power over me. I am covered by the blood of Jesus.

1 Peter 2:10 (KJV): "Which in time past were not a people, but are now the people of God: which had not obtained mercy, but now have obtained mercy."

3. I am the righteousness of God in Christ Jesus. Shame, reproach, condemnation, and false labels have been stripped away from my life. I am clothed with the garment of Christ and reflect Him in all my actions. I am a new creation.

2 Corinthians 5:17 (KJV): "Therefore, if anyone is in Christ, he is a new creation; old things have passed away; behold, all things have become new."

4. Father, awaken the gifts within me and let them flow through my entire being. Grant me the strength and wisdom to use them wisely and effectively for Your glory in Jesus' name.

1 Peter 4:10 (NLT): "God has given each of you a gift from His great variety of spiritual gifts. Use them well to serve one another."

5. Lord, I declare that my mind is free from every captivity that has held me down. I receive the strength to align with Your Word until I become the

Word. From today, I see myself as Your chosen vessel on earth and exercise the authority given to me through the blood of Jesus Christ.

Luke 10:19 (KJV): "Behold, I give unto you the power to tread on serpents and scorpions, and over all the power of the enemy: and nothing shall by any means hurt you."

6. Father, I repent of any offence or disobedience in carrying out my assignment because of anger or intolerance. I receive the patience to be considerate, slow to anger, and to apply wisdom through the Holy Spirit whenever I feel challenged.

Galatians 5:22-23 (KJV):"But the fruit of the Spirit is love, joy, peace, longsuffering, gentleness, goodness, faith, meekness, temperance: against such there is no law."

7. Father, I submit my soul to You. Expose any stronghold in my life and wash me with Your blood. Create in me a clean heart and renew my spirit.

Psalm 51:10-12 (KJV): "Create in me a clean heart, O God; and renew a right spirit within me. Cast me not away from Your presence; and take not Your Holy Spirit from me. Restore unto me the joy of Your salvation, and uphold me with Your free spirit."

8. Lord, I receive deliverance from pornography, the lust of the flesh, stubbornness, pride, and spiritual blindness. Guide me on the right path so I may walk in righteousness.

Psalm 107:7 (KJV): "And He led them forth by the right way, that they might go to a city of habitation."

9. Thank You, Lord, for redeeming me from every curse. I walk in the freedom Christ has given me.

Galatians 3:13 (KJV): "Christ has redeemed us from the curse of the law, having become a curse for us (for it is written, 'Cursed is everyone who hangs on a tree')."

10. Father, I declare that my steps are ordered by You. I will not walk in confusion or fear but in

divine direction. I trust in Your leading as I fulfil my purpose.

Psalm 37:23 (KJV): "The steps of a good man are ordered by the Lord: and he delighteth in his way."

Keep declaring these truths until they become your reality. Your voice activates your destiny, and with God, all things are possible!

CLOSING PRAYER

Heavenly Father, I thank You for this new beginning. I receive the grace to fulfil my divine assignment on earth. I declare that every door the enemy has used to gain access to me is now closed forever, in Jesus' name. Amen

CHAPTER TWO
NOW THE WAR BEGINS:
THE STAR WATCHERS

"The devil does not attack the ordinary; he fights the extraordinary. The moment you carry a divine assignment, you become a target." - Esther Samson

ANCHOR SCRIPTURE

"For we are not fighting against people made of flesh and blood, but against the evil rulers and authorities of the unseen world, against those

mighty powers of darkness who rule this world, and against wicked spirits in the heavenly realms." - Ephesians 6:12 (NLT)

The dark forces are aware when a chosen one is about to be born, and they will do everything in their power to stop the child.

The battle over your life did not start today. It began the moment God marked you for greatness.

This chapter shares insights and references from the lives of Jesus and Mary, as well as my experiences, highlighting the many tactics the devil uses to prevent you from fulfilling your divine assignment on earth.

MARY: THE CHOSEN ONE

Mary, from the royal lineage of David (Luke 3:23-38), was a relative of Elizabeth, who belonged to the priestly line of Aaron (Luke 1:5, 36). This connection highlights both royal and priestly heritage in the unfolding of God's divine plan.

Mary's pivotal role in the birth of Jesus was even foretold by the Prophet Isaiah: *"Therefore the Lord Himself shall give you a sign; Behold, a virgin shall conceive, and bear a son, and shall call his name Immanuel." (Isaiah 7:14, KJV)*

From the moment Mary was born, she was a chosen vessel, destined to bring forth Immanuel—Jesus Christ, the Son of God. He is God in human form, sent to bring redemption to the world. Though she did not enter the world adorned in gold and her appearance was ordinary, she was uniquely suited for a monumental purpose that would change the course of history.

This divine selection became evident when the angel Gabriel appeared to her with a life-altering message: *"And in the sixth month the angel Gabriel was sent from God unto a city of Galilee, named Nazareth, to a virgin espoused to a man whose name was Joseph, of the house of David; and the virgin's name was Mary. And the angel came in unto her, and said, Hail, thou that art highly favoured, the Lord is with thee: blessed art thou among women." (Luke 1:26-28, KJV)*

Mary's journey was not just one of divine favour but of great responsibility. Though she was an ordinary young woman in the eyes of many, she was chosen by God for an extraordinary purpose—to carry the Saviour of the world.

THE KINGDOM OF DARKNESS IS THREATENED BY LIGHT

Matthew 2:1-6 (NLT) says, *"Jesus was born in Bethlehem in Judea, during the reign of King Herod. About that time, some wise men from eastern lands arrived in Jerusalem, asking, 'Where is the newborn King of the Jews? We saw his star as it rose, and we have come to worship him.' King Herod was deeply disturbed when he heard this, as was everyone in Jerusalem. He called a meeting of the leading priests and teachers of religious law and asked, 'Where is the Messiah supposed to be born?' 'In Bethlehem in Judea,' they said, 'for this is what the prophet wrote: 'And you, O Bethlehem, in the land of Judah, are not least among the ruling cities of Judah; for a ruler will come from you who will be the shepherd for my people Israel.'"*

In the Book of Matthew, as cited above, when King Herod heard the news of Jesus' imminent birth, he sought to kill Him. However, God granted Joseph and Mary the wisdom to hide the Messiah, who was destined to save humanity.

Matthew 2:13-15 (NLT) says, "After the wise men were gone, an angel of the Lord appeared to Joseph in a dream. 'Get up! Flee to Egypt with the child and his mother,' the angel said. 'Stay there until I tell you to return because Herod is going to search for the child to kill him.' That night, Joseph left for Egypt with the child and Mary, his mother, and they stayed there until Herod's death. This fulfilled what the Lord had spoken through the prophet: 'I called my Son out of Egypt.'"

Herod, driven by a thirst for power, feared anything that threatened his reign. Historical accounts reveal that he even murdered several of his family members, whom he suspected of plotting against him, demonstrating the extent of his cruelty.

When light shines, darkness must retreat. Jesus embodied that light, ready to lift the veil of darkness from the eyes of many, which is why Herod sought to stop Him. Similarly, God has chosen you to carry out His purpose in a specific area or more.

While the devil may try to challenge you, always remember that God has already triumphed over the world. With Him, nothing is beyond reach. So even in your persecution, rejoice because the war has already been won. John 16:33 (NIRV) says, *"I have told you these things so that you can have peace because of me. In this world, you will have trouble. But be encouraged! I have won the battle over the world."*

THE FIGHT IS NOT OF THE FLESH—WAR FOR YOUR DESTINY!

After I received Jesus Christ as my Lord and Saviour, my mother enrolled me in a discipleship class that met every Saturday. It was a good experience. I would sit through various activities— some I fully understood, while others left me puzzled.

Yet, it felt as if unseen forces were trying to hold me back from stepping into my authority in Christ. The discipleship class often seemed more like a Bible story session, and while I genuinely enjoyed it, something still felt missing. I memorized numerous Bible verses and graduated from the program, but deep inside, I knew I had not grasped the true essence of my faith.

Then came boarding school — and that was when the nightmare began. I vividly recall a disturbing dream in which a woman chased me and forced me to eat something. The next morning, I woke up coughing up blood. My condition worsened so severely that my mother had to take me out of school. The doctor diagnosed me with tuberculosis, but I had no idea how or where I had contracted it.

In that terrifying moment, I realized I had no power to pray or assert my authority in Christ. All I had was the knowledge of being baptized — I thought that was enough. My mother, desperate for my healing, took me to the hospital while reaching out to several pastors to pray for my recovery.

Before I returned to school, I began studying the Word of God on my own. It became clear that my life had become a target for the kingdom of darkness. My mother encouraged me to memorize and recite Psalms 91 and 23 whenever I felt threatened. *"Even when I walk through the darkest valley, I will not be afraid, for you are close beside me. Your rod and your staff protect and comfort me." (Psalm 23:4, NLT).*

At 13, my school planned an end-of-term party. My roommates urged me not to go, but I was determined to have fun. I dived into the pool, laughing and splashing around with the other girls. But suddenly, I felt something pulling me towards the deep end. In an instant, I began to drown.

My life flashed before my eyes—I even saw the smile of my baby brother. In my desperation, I cried out, "Jesus, save me!" Just then, someone pulled me from the water. As I was resuscitated, I could not help but wonder—who had saved me? No one else had seen this person.

Later, I came to understand the spiritual warfare at play in my life. *"Dear friends, don't be surprised at the fiery trials you are going through, as if something strange were happening to you." (1 Peter 4:12, NLT).* The enemy had set traps for me, but God had been my rescue.

Yet, despite this miraculous deliverance, the devil had succeeded in planting seeds of doubt in my heart. I did not feel set apart or chosen. Instead, I wondered, why must I suffer so much? What is wrong with me?

The doubt buried itself deep within me, slowly taking root. Little did I know, it would become a tool the enemy would use to make me question my identity in Christ.

THE CHOSEN CAN BECOME A CONTAMINATED SEED

That same year that God saved me from drowning, my parents went their separate ways after being together for 20 years. It was during this difficult time that my classmates introduced me to pornography, marking the beginning of a silent struggle.

I was never genuinely drawn to what I saw, yet that moment cracked open a door in my life—one the devil exploited to keep me trapped and undermine my sense of worthiness for my kingdom assignment. I later realized that when someone decides to follow Jesus, they become a target for the forces of darkness. These principalities work tirelessly to plant seeds of doubt about your faith, identity, and the authority that Jesus Christ has given you. The aim is to contaminate the seed in you so that you grow to become tainted.

This strategy mirrors that of the serpent in the Garden of Eden—his goal was to create a rift between humanity and God, making people believe they were permanently fallen and unworthy of redemption. But that is not the final chapter of our story. God sent Jesus Christ to change the narrative, and through His blood, we have been adopted into His Kingdom as sons and daughters. Therefore, we have found

REDEMPTION.

Romans 8:15 reminds us of this truth: *"For ye have not received the spirit of bondage again to fear; but ye have received the Spirit of adoption, whereby we cry, Abba, Father."*

No matter how stained we may feel, God's grace is greater. As Romans 3:24 (KJV) declares, *"Being justified freely by His grace through the redemption that is in Christ Jesus." Through Jesus, we are redeemed, restored, and made new.*

A GOD OF SECOND CHANCES

Lucifer seeks to sabotage your calling because it holds the power to influence not only your life but also the lives of those around you. Your calling is a channel for spreading God's goodness and helping others discover their purpose.

This is exactly why the enemy works tirelessly to prevent your destiny from flourishing. He aims to disrupt every step you take, trying to divert you from God's plan for your life. But here is the reality: Jesus has already overcome these obstacles—let this truth be your anchor.

My foundation in Christ was not strong for a long time, which held me back from fully embracing my calling. I read the Bible and attended church, but I did not understand God's Word, nor could I fully live by His truth. My mind was captive to confusion. Yet, God never lost faith in me. The purpose God has placed in your life is the exact reason the devil will stop at nothing to thwart you.

As John 10:10 (NLT) says: *"The thief's purpose is to steal and kill and destroy. My purpose is to give them a rich and satisfying life."* The enemy aims to steal your joy and peace, but Jesus came to give you an abundant life, a life of purpose and fulfilment.

When I graduated from secondary school, my future seemed bright. I had planned to study visual communication at a university in Baltimore, secure a great job in a corporation, and eventually marry. Unfortunately, my hopes were dashed when my visa application was denied, which meant I could not enrol at the university. The thought of spending the next four years at home felt unbearable.

However, a friend suggested I apply to Igbinedion University in Okada, Edo State, Nigeria. My mother prayed fervently, and after much faith, I received the admission letter. Just when I was on the verge of depression, God's light began to shine through my situation, leading to my acceptance at the university.

From my first year to my last, I developed a deep passion for helping others and nurturing a love for humanity and the Gospel. But just before graduation, another challenge arose that tested my faith.

After enjoying a meal prepared by a friend, I suddenly found myself rushed to the emergency room, my body on the verge of shutting down. The doctor confirmed I had been poisoned. My roommate, who had eaten the same meal, was in tears and utterly confused, yet she showed no signs of illness. We quickly called our youth pastor, who arrived and sensed that dark forces were at play.

He began to pray, and I felt an intense burning sensation. Some witnesses later said they saw fire surrounding the room. It felt surreal, like something out of a fantasy movie, but who can underestimate God—Yeshua. That night, I was miraculously delivered from death. Yet, my faith had been shaken again.

GOD LOVES HIS AMBASSADORS

It is clear that despite the snares laid by the devil for those called by God, our Father will always remain a refuge for His children. Whether in a firestorm or after a shipwreck, He stands on the shore with an outstretched hand, encouraging us not to lose hope, no matter the circumstances. This is why He urges us to view life through the lens of faith, letting His love and Spirit guide us.

Seeing through the eyes of faith is essential because God can do anything. Romans 8:28 (KJV) reminds us, *"And we know that all things work together for good to them that love God, to them who are called according to His purpose."* This verse assures us that, no matter the trials, God works everything for the good of those who love Him and are called according to His purpose.

God's ambassadors are individuals whom God has called to carry out His purpose on earth. They are meant to represent Him, spread His message, and make a difference in the world through their lives, actions, and faith. Many of these ambassador's face struggles and challenges. Some have even turned away from their calling, believing that following God means enduring endless trials. And while answering God's call does come with responsibilities and challenges, it is important to remember that God is always with us.

You may face persecution, hatred, and attacks from dark forces. Friends and family may abandon you, and you might make choices that threaten to shake your faith. But I have been in that dark hole, and trust me, it is not a place I wish for anyone. Yet, God's love never fails, and He covers you. He desires you to remain connected to Him by deepening your faith, immersing yourself in His Word, and nurturing your spirit.

DECLARATIONS

1. I receive the keys to the kingdom of heaven to prevail over the gates of hell.

Matthew 16:17-19 (KJV): "And Jesus answered and said unto him, Blessed art thou, Simon Barjona: for flesh and blood hath not revealed it unto thee, but my Father which is in heaven. And I say also unto thee, That thou art Peter, and upon this rock I will build my church; and the gates of hell shall not prevail against it. And I will give unto thee the keys of the kingdom of heaven: and whatsoever thou shalt bind on earth shall be bound in heaven: and whatsoever thou shalt loose on earth shall be loosed in heaven."

2. I submit to Your will so that You can do Your work through me in the name of Jesus.

Philippians 2:13 (NLT): "For God is working in you, giving you the desire and the power to do what pleases Him."

3. Jesus has won the battle, and I overcome every accuser by the blood of the Lamb.

Revelation 12:11 (KJV): "And they overcame him by the blood of the Lamb, and by the word of their testimony, and they loved not their lives unto the death."

4. Father, thank You for calling me into Your Kingdom and erasing my shame.

Isaiah 54:4 (NLT): "Fear not; you will no longer live in

shame. Don't be afraid; there is no more disgrace for you. You will no longer remember the shame of your youth and the sorrows of widowhood."

5. I choose to walk daily in Your grace because Jesus Christ has made me perfect despite my weaknesses.

2 Corinthians 12:9 (KJV): "And He said unto me, My grace is sufficient for thee: for my strength is made perfect in weakness. Most gladly, therefore, will I rather glory in my infirmities, that the power of Christ may rest upon me."

6. I silence every battle over my call. Thank You for being my rock and training me to war for all You have called me to do.

Psalm 144:1 (KJV): "Blessed be the Lord my strength, which teacheth my hands to war, and my fingers to fight."

7. I am more than a conqueror and will succeed in all I do. I will no longer experience demonic delays or frustrations in Jesus' name.

Romans 8:37 (KJV): "Nay, in all these things we are more than conquerors through Him that loved us."

8. Lord, You are my peace. No matter the challenges I face during my assignment, I will remain steadfast, holding onto Your hands to direct me in Jesus' name.

John 16:33 (KJV): "These things I have spoken unto you, that in me ye might have peace. In the world ye shall have tribulation: but be of good cheer; I have overcome the world."

9. In everything I do, I will lean on Your understanding and not mine in Jesus' name.

Proverbs 3:5-6 (KJV): "Trust in the Lord with all thine heart, and lean not unto thine own understanding. In all thy ways acknowledge Him, and He shall direct thy paths."

10. Father, I thank You because every war is over. The former things are forgotten and erased by the

blood of Jesus. Every negative experience is wiped clean from my bloodstream. I am a new creation ready for the task before me.

2 Corinthians 5:17 (KJV): "Therefore if any man is in Christ, he is a new creature: old things are passed away; behold, all things become new."

11. The Lord is with me, a mighty warrior. He has subdued the enemies targeting my calling. I am victorious in Jesus' name.

Jeremiah 20:11 (KJV): "But the Lord is with me as a mighty terrible one: therefore my persecutors shall stumble, and they shall not prevail: they shall be greatly ashamed; for they shall not prosper: their everlasting confusion shall never be forgotten."

CLOSING PRAYER

Father, I thank You because every battle over my divine assignment has already been won on the cross. Thank You, Lord, for saving me and granting me another opportunity to complete all that You have called me to do on earth. The enemy will no longer cause me to stray, in Jesus' name. Amen.

CHAPTER THREE
THE FIRST AWAKENING: HOW I BECAME DEEPLY AWARE OF GOD'S CALL ON MY LIFE

"Sometimes, God shakes us to awaken us. The wake-up call may be painful, but it is always purposeful." - Esther Samson

ANCHOR SCRIPTURE

"I pray that God, the source of hope, will fill you completely with joy and peace because you trust in

Him. Then you will overflow with confident hope through the power of the Holy Spirit." - Romans 15:13 (NLT)

I did not wake up to my true identity in Christ all at once. It took moments of struggle, pain, and deep longing for something more—something real.

Faith is the substance of things hoped for, and by faith, we receive Jesus Christ, die with Him, and are resurrected with Him (Hebrews 11:1-3). However, I did not fully walk in this understanding. I lived a life with one foot in Christ and the other in the world, which is why I constantly faced backlash from the enemy. But despite this, God still gave me another chance.

2013

In 2013, I faced challenges that forced me to take a deep look at my life. I was trapped in the weight of childhood trauma, a broken marriage, infertility, poverty, and an overwhelming sense of hopelessness. I often wondered: "Does God really love me?"

I had married someone who did not share my faith, believing I could change him. But the marriage crumbled, and instead of finding support from the church members I trusted, I felt shunned and abandoned. The pain was unbearable, and doubts began to consume me—doubts about God, about my worth, and about whether my life even mattered. At my lowest, I considered ending it all.

Yet, somehow, I clung to a thread of hope. Desperate for direction, I applied for vocational training, hoping it would give my life some purpose. I went through the motions—waking up for prayer and attending church every Sunday—yet my heart remained distant from God.

Bitterness grew within me. I resented my ex-husband, the people who had failed me, and the life I was living. Slowly, I became a shadow of myself, trapped in a cycle of pain, unable to see a way forward.

2AM WAKE-UP CALL

"Esther, will you do My work?" I heard those words three times around 2 am one morning and wondered who was speaking to me—until I heard them again. Still half-asleep, I responded, "Lord, You know I have my issues, and as a single mother, I just can't handle the work right now."

That was the last time I would hear the Lord speak so clearly to me, and it became my first awakening.

LOST IN THE PRISON OF EXCUSES

Life seemed to move quickly. I graduated from vocational training, juggled multiple jobs, and even wrote my first book in German. I thought this was all that God had planned for me, but deep down, I knew there was more. Yet, I kept making excuses that held me back.

Perhaps you have also had those quiet moments—late at night or early in the morning—when you sensed a divine call, just as I did. In those moments, it is easy to list reasons why you are not the right person for the task: "Lord, I can't speak well. Have you seen how I look? I don't have any money. The people you want me to reach are hypocrites, vain, and involved in all sorts of wrongdoings. I can't step into the political arena—I fear for my safety, and what would other Christians think?"

Excuses can pile up, trapping you in a false reality where you assume tomorrow will bring the same opportunities. But while God is patient, He will move on and find others if you choose to rely on your excuses instead of trusting Him. If you are not careful, excuses can push you into regret, missed opportunities, and spiritual stagnation.

DECLARATIONS

1. Father, help me to own up to my responsibilities. I receive the strength to represent You rightly at the places You send me.

Exodus 4:10-14 (NLT): "But Moses pleaded with the Lord, "O Lord, I'm not very good with words. I never have been, and I'm not now, even though You have spoken to me. I get tongue-tied, and my words get tangled." Then the Lord asked Moses, "Who makes a person's mouth? Who decides whether people speak or do not speak, hear or do not hear, see or do not see? Is it not I, the Lord? Now go! I will be with you as you speak, and I will instruct you on what to say." But Moses again pleaded, "Lord, please! Send anyone else." Then the Lord became angry with Moses. "All right," He said. "What about your brother, Aaron the Levite? I know he speaks well. And look! He is on his way to meet you now. He will be delighted to see you."

2. Lord, I receive deliverance from the veil of ignorance. From today, I will no longer do things out of ignorance. I come out of every slumber of darkness in Jesus' name.

Ephesians 4:18 (NLT): "Their minds are full of darkness; they wander far from the life God gives because they have closed their minds and hardened their hearts against Him."

3. Lord, open my heart so I can understand and discern when You speak to me.

John 10:27 (NLT): "My sheep listen to my voice; I know them, and they follow me."

4. In everything I do, I will be led by the Spirit of God and not by my flesh. I take my position as Your son/daughter.

Romans 8:14-17 (NLT): "For all who are led by the Spirit of God are children of God. So you have not received a spirit that makes you fearful slaves. Instead, you received God's Spirit when He adopted you as His own children. Now we call Him, "Abba, Father." For His Spirit joins with our spirit to affirm that we are God's children. And since we are His children, we are His heirs. In fact, together with Christ, we are heirs of God's glory. But if we are to share His glory, we must also share His suffering."

5. Father, thank You for giving me a heart that will continue to yearn for You deeply in Jesus' name.

Psalm 42:1 (NLT): "As the deer longs for streams of water, so I long for You, O God."

6. I receive the power of resurrection in the name of Jesus. From today, nothing dies in my hands.

John 11:25 (NLT): "Jesus told her, "I am the resurrection and the life. Anyone who believes in Me will live, even after dying."

7. Lord, thank You for awakening my soul from every trap of slumber in Jesus' name.

1 Thessalonians 5:6 (NLT): "So be on your guard, not asleep like the others. Stay alert and be clearheaded."

8. Father, in Your grace, I find Your face. I will continue to hold onto Your truth in Jesus' name.

Hebrews 4:16 (NLT): "So let us come boldly to the throne of our gracious God. There we will receive His mercy, and we will find grace to help us when we need it most."

9. Today, I walk with eagle's wings in the name of Jesus.

Isaiah 40:31 (NLT): "But those who trust in the Lord will find new strength. They will soar high on wings like eagles. They will run and not grow weary. They will walk and not faint."

10. Father, thank You for this transformation and for giving me the sight to see myself the way You see

me. Thank You for anointing my head with Your oil. I am awakened in Your righteousness in Jesus' name. Amen.

Psalm 23:5 (NLT): "You prepare a feast for me in the presence of my enemies. You honour me by anointing my head with oil. My cup overflows with blessings."

CLOSING PRAYER

Father, I thank You for restoring me to Yourself. I will no longer live in disobedience or be double-minded. As Your Word says in Lamentations 5:21 (NLT): "Restore us, O Lord, and bring us back to You again! Give us back the joys we once had!" Amen.

CHAPTER FOUR
THE PRODIGAL DAUGHTER

"You can appear whole on the outside, yet be broken within. True restoration begins when you submit to the One who created you." - Esther Samson

ANCHOR SCRIPTURE

"That is why those who are still under the control of their sinful nature can never please God." –
Romans 8:8 (NLT)

Have you ever chased after something, believing it would bring you happiness, only to realize you were actually drifting further from God?

That was my reality. I thought I was pursuing success, freedom, and a fulfilling life, but the truth is, I was running away from the only One who could truly satisfy my soul.

To walk in God's calling for your life, you must learn to see the world through His eyes. But after my last encounter with God, I lost sight of that. Instead of pursuing His will, I became consumed with the mindset of "Get rich or die trying."

Nothing else mattered—not even the path of the kingdom. I kept chasing what I thought was right, yet I was left with an emptiness I could not explain. I felt like I was merely surviving. Anger and bitterness gradually took root in my heart, consuming me from within.

I was constantly agitated and at war with myself. These emotions opened doors for the enemy to sow thorns into every area of my life. Ironically, despite the inner turmoil, I maintained a beautiful facade. The world saw a polished exterior, but beneath it, I was crumbling under the weight of my disobedience.

THE LONG WAY HOME

After attending an end-of-the-year service at my old church, I knew it was time to leave for a new Bethel in Duisburg, Germany. At the church, I met my pastor, who trained me in sharing the Gospel and interpreting the prophetic dreams I was having. God was also using me in areas of dream building and encouragement.

However, despite all this, I still struggled to walk truly in my calling. I could not let go of my past or fully see myself as an adopted daughter in God's kingdom. Shame from past mistakes constantly weighed me down, and no matter how hard God tried to pull me into His light, the darkness seemed to pull me towards itself.

For over four years, I struggled with my training. I can honestly say there were times when I left my training ground because my flesh was stronger than my spirit. This happens when we feed our bodies with the wrong things. As Romans 13:14 (KJV) says, *"But put ye on the Lord Jesus Christ, and make not provision for the flesh, to fulfil the lusts thereof."*

I remember starting the prophetic class with my pastor, but I just could not focus. Then, I discovered my love for singing. Whenever I sang, there was a prophetic anointing, and some members of our church testified to experiencing healing through it. Yet, I continued to make excuses and often did not show up for practice. Maybe I was too tired or too ashamed because I was a divorced single mother. I felt unworthy and sometimes, I would ask myself, "Why would God choose someone like me?"

There were times when I felt God waking me up in the middle of the night to pray, but my flesh would not allow me to obey. I ignored the call and, in doing so, hindered my growth.

Despite my resistance, God never left me. There are many believers whom God has called to occupy positions around the world, yet the flesh and lack of self-understanding often stand as obstacles to answering the call.

For years, I could not fulfil God's assignment or go where He wanted me to go because I did not see myself as worthy. I was coming from a place of trauma, shame, and rejection, and I kept wondering who would accept me or how I could possibly represent God on earth.

But Colossians 2:6-7 (NLT) reminds us: *"And now, just as you accepted Christ Jesus as your Lord, you must continue to follow Him. Let your roots grow down into Him, and let your lives be built on Him. Then your faith will grow strong in the truth you were taught, and you will overflow with thankfulness."*

God's grace is available to all. We are no longer bound by the law. Don't let the devil or religious figures deceive you. God has a plan for you, and His grace empowers you to walk in your calling.

GETTING OUT OF THE STRUGGLE PHASE: EXERCISE

To overcome the struggle phase in fulfilling God's calling on your life, spend more time with God through quiet time, prayer, fasting, and speaking with believers who reflect Jesus. Seek clarity on what exactly He is calling you to do, write it down, and start taking actions to make it a reality.

See beyond your weaknesses, mistakes, and traumatic pasts that have opened the door to shame and rejection. Hold on to God's grace. Invite the Holy Spirit to take over your life and give you a new understanding of who you are and who God has called you to be.

Equip yourself with the Word of God, which is the truth and the life. Confess Jesus daily and understand that you are in covenant with Him through His Blood. The old you no longer exist.

Walk by faith. Just as the disciples spread the Gospel and represented Jesus Christ through belief, it is with your faith in Yahweh that you can walk in your calling—not by your strength.

Everything may try to disqualify you: your past, the voice of society, modern-day Pharisees, principalities, and powers. But your BELIEF IN

JESUS CHRIST should be your anchor, standing firm against negative whispers.

DECLARATIONS

1. I am now in Christ Jesus. Therefore, I silence every voice of the accuser. I silence the voice of shame, regret, trauma, and mistakes from my past. In Jesus, I am free.

Romans 8:1-4 (KJV): "There is therefore now no condemnation to them which are in Christ Jesus, who walk not after the flesh, but after the Spirit. For the law of the Spirit of life in Christ Jesus hath made me free from the law of sin and death. For what the law could not do, in that it was weak through the flesh, God sent his own Son in the likeness of sinful flesh, and for sin, condemned sin in the flesh: That the righteousness of the law might be fulfilled in us, who walk not after the flesh, but after the Spirit."

2. God has called me by name and everything I do will be for His Glory.

Isaiah 43:7 (NLT): "Bring all who claim me as their God, for I have made them for my glory. It was I who created them."

3. I walk in the understanding of redemption through the blood of Jesus Christ. The devil will no longer remind me of my past. The mercy of Jesus speaks through me.

Ephesians 1:7 (NLT): "He is so rich in kindness and grace that He purchased our freedom with the blood of His Son and forgave our sins."

4. Father, my unrighteousness has been pardoned in the name of Jesus. I will no longer be disobedient to Your voice.

Psalm 32:1 (KJV): "Blessed is he whose transgression is forgiven, whose sin is covered."

5. Father, thank You for demonstrating Your love for me through Your Son. I am forever loved and will hold onto this love as I carry out my assignment.

Romans 5:8 (KJV): "But God commendeth His love toward us, in that, while we were yet sinners, Christ died for us."

CLOSING PRAYER

Father, I surrender my will, my soul, and everything to You. I will no longer wrestle with You concerning my calling. I repent of every action that has led me to abandon what You have appointed me to do in Jesus' name. Amen.

CHAPTER FIVE
BEYOND THE PULPIT

"God's calling is not confined to the pulpit; it is a mandate to influence the world with His light — wherever you are." - Esther Samson

ANCHOR SCRIPTURES

"And hath made us kings and priests unto God and His Father; to Him be glory and dominion forever and ever. Amen." **- Revelation 1:6 (KJV)**

"And He gave some, apostles; and some, prophets; and some, evangelists; and some, pastors and teachers." - **Ephesians 4:11 (KJV)**

For too long, we have boxed God's call into the narrow space of the pulpit. Many believe that divine assignment means becoming a pastor, but God's purpose extends far beyond the four walls of the church. Think about Joseph, Daniel, and Esther—they were not preachers behind a pulpit, yet they carried God's influence into governance, leadership, and national transformation.

Could it be that the reason you have not answered your call is because, deep down, you know God is calling you to something bigger than a title? Maybe your hesitation comes from feeling unqualified, past regrets, or fear of stepping into the unknown. But hear this—God has been preparing you all along. The struggles, the training, the disappointments, and the lessons are not wasted.

It is time to rise. The world needs kingdom-minded leaders in business, government, media, education, and every sphere of influence. The fire has refined you. Now, you are ready!

DANIEL AS A CASE STUDY

Daniel, a descendant of Judah's royal family, was selected to serve under the administration of King Nebuchadnezzar. In modern terms, he could be considered a political adviser to the president of a nation.

Gifted in the prophetic, Daniel could interpret dreams through the Spirit of God in him. He accurately predicted the rise and fall of the Greek and Roman Empires (Daniel 11:2-4, Daniel 2:19-23, Daniel 2:27-28, Daniel 6:3) and prophesied about the Messiah who would be killed (Daniel 9:24-27). His prophetic gift and wise counsel played a crucial role in saving the king during his time.

God strategically placed Daniel in a circle of unbelievers. This might seem unusual, as many believe that God's calling is limited to the four walls of the church. However, Daniel's unwavering dedication to God brought both opportunities and opposition. His colleagues conspired against him, leading to his imprisonment in the lion's den. Yet, God miraculously shut the mouths of the lions, leaving Daniel unharmed. Through this event, God's power was revealed, compelling unbelievers to acknowledge Him.

The story of Daniel reinforces the truth: God's calling is diverse—it extends beyond the pulpit. God can call anyone to any sphere of influence across the globe. Therefore, remain open and discerning, seeing through His eyes to understand where He is leading you. His ways are not our ways.

STEPPING OUT OF YOUR COMFORT ZONE WITH COURAGE

It is easy to sit behind your computer, switch on your Facebook Live, and share God's word or whatever He has called you to do from the comfort of your home. However, God often calls us beyond the four corners of our homes.

Recently, I heard a woman speak about the Lord sending her to one of the countries in the Middle East to comfort Christian widows and young girls. These women are often marginalized and abused due to their faith.

For her family, this was a huge risk because Christians are widely hated in the country, but one thing is sure: when God calls you, He sends His angels ahead of you, encompassing you with His presence.

After Moses' death, God spoke to Joshua, knowing his capacity and the state of his heart. He encouraged him to hold onto His word, giving him specific instructions on what to do. God helped Joshua and the Israelites cross the River Jordan, and the Amorite Kings were paralyzed with fear when they heard what had happened.

Joshua 1:9 (NLT): *"This is my command—be strong and courageous! Do not be afraid or discouraged. For the Lord your God is with you wherever you go."*

God is calling you beyond your comfort zone. You are one of His chosen superheroes for a time like this. He wants to use the abilities He has deposited in you for the advancement of His kingdom, but you must step out of your comfort zone and rely on His courage to answer His call.

It might be as simple as praying for your father, who you have struggled to forgive. God wants you to forgive your family so that He can use you to bring

His gift of salvation to them.

It might be that He is calling you to help children from broken homes, teaching them the difference between God's love and worldly love. He wants them to find healing through the abilities He has given them. That is why you must step out of your comfort zone to answer the call.

DECLARATIONS

1. Father, I pray that You strengthen me with boldness and courage. Help me to be strong and courageous, knowing that You are with me wherever I go. I will not fear or be discouraged, for You are my God, and I trust in Your presence to guide me every step of the way.

Joshua 1:9 (NLT): "This is my command—be strong and courageous! Do not be afraid or discouraged. For the Lord your God is with you wherever you go."

2. Lord, I trust in Your perfect plan for my life, even when it takes me out of my comfort zone. I believe that You have good plans for me, plans to prosper me and give me hope. Help me to rest in the assurance that You are in control and that You will lead me to where You want me to be.

Jeremiah 29:11 (KJV): "For I know the thoughts that I think towards you, saith the Lord, thoughts of peace, and not of evil, to give you an expected end."

3. Father, I surrender to Your call. I am ready to obey and walk in the direction You are leading me. Just as You called Isaiah, I, too, say, "Here am I. Send me!" Equip me with everything I need to fulfil the purpose You have placed in my heart. Let my life be a testament to Your glory.

Isaiah 6:8 (KJV): "Also I heard the voice of the Lord, saying, Whom shall I send, and who will go for us? Then said I, 'Here am I; send me."'

4. Lord, I pray for Your divine protection as I step out in faith. I trust that Your angels are surrounding me, keeping me safe from harm and guiding me along the path You have set before me. Thank You for watching over me and for going ahead of me in every situation.

Psalm 91:11 (NLT): "For He will order His angels to protect you wherever you go."

5. Heavenly Father, I trust that You will provide everything I need to fulfil Your calling on my life. I believe that You will supply all my needs according to Your glorious riches in Christ Jesus. Help me to rely on Your provision and to walk in faith, knowing that You will never leave me without providing what I need.

Philippians 4:19 (KJV): "But my God shall supply all your needs according to his riches in glory by Christ Jesus."

CLOSING PRAYER

Father, thank You for calling me to be part of Your great plan for this world. I know that You are always with me, guiding me and equipping me for the journey ahead. I ask for the courage to step out of my comfort zone and to boldly answer Your call.

Strengthen me to forgive, to love, and to serve those You have placed in my path. Let Your presence go before me, and may Your angels surround me as I walk in obedience. Help me to trust in Your plan, knowing that You have a purpose for me that is greater than I can see in Jesus' name. Amen.

CHAPTER SIX

THE TRAINING SEASON

"God's training ground may not always be comfortable, but it is always necessary. The depth of your preparation determines the height of your impact." - Esther Samson

ANCHOR SCRIPTURE

"No training seems pleasant at the time. In fact, it seems painful. But later on, it produces a harvest of godliness and peace. It does that for those who have been trained by it." - Hebrews 12:11 (NIRV)

Have you ever wondered why soldiers go through intense training before they are sent to battle? It is because no one is sent to war unprepared. The training may be tough, painful, and sometimes overwhelming, but it equips them to survive and win.

In the same way, God never sends His people out without preparation. He takes them through seasons of training, shaping them for the assignment ahead. If you resist the process, you will find yourself unprepared when the challenges arise. But when you embrace it, you gain the wisdom, strength, and endurance needed to fulfil your purpose.

THE PURPOSE OF TRAINING

Training is rarely enjoyable in the moment, but it is essential for growth. Sometimes, it begins before the call; other times, it happens within the call itself. One thing is certain—it never truly stops. If you miss your training season, you will lack the essential tools needed to fulfil your destiny.

THE DANGERS OF IGNORING TRAINING

Imagine a soldier heading to war without a bulletproof vest, ammunition, medication, night goggles, or a communication device. What would happen when he faces the enemy? He would likely become an easy target.

In the same way, skipping your training season makes you vulnerable. Many people desire the glory of their calling but resist the refining process that precedes it. Without training, even the most gifted person can fall apart when challenges arise.

TRAINING THROUGH BIBLICAL EXAMPLES

Jesus, the Son of God, went through years of preparation before stepping into His divine assignment. Luke 2:46 tells us, *"After three days they found Him in the temple courts, sitting among the teachers, listening to them and asking them questions."* Jesus spent years learning, growing, and preparing before stepping into ministry at age 30, which lasted only three and a half years. Isn't that amazing?

Similarly, Ehud, the deliverer of Israel, was called to assassinate King Eglon of Moab at a time of distress (Judges 3:12-30). Though the Bible does not tell us if he was a trained soldier, it is evident that God had been preparing him for that moment. His ability to execute the mission successfully was a result of divine training long before he stepped into his assignment.

God's training process is intentional. It may be tough, and it may not always make sense at the moment, but it is designed to prepare you for the journey ahead. If you embrace your training season, you will be equipped for the assignment God has called you to. Don't despise the process; it is shaping you for greatness.

GETTING THE BEST OUT OF THE TRAINING SEASON

God loves intimacy. Whether through praise, prayer, fasting, silent meditation on His Word, or simply showing up and saying, "Lord, here I am. Let your perfect will be done in my life," God desires a deeper relationship with you. He wants you to trust Him with your whole being. During your training season, make it a priority to sit at His feet. Spend more time in His presence so He can reveal the mysteries of your calling to you.

To get the best out of the training season, you must feast on God's Word. Jesus emphasized the importance of knowing the Scriptures when He said in Matthew 22:29 (KJV): *"Jesus answered and said unto them, Ye do err, not knowing the scriptures, nor the power of God."*

Scripture is a guide that helps you rediscover God's vision for your life. Through His Word, He activates truth and light in you. The lives of Jesus, Abraham, Moses, David, and Elijah reveal a common principle—consistent intimacy with God. They repeatedly sought God for divine instructions concerning their calling. They often asked, "Father, what next? How? When? What do You want me to do? Or am I simply here to enjoy Your presence?"

David understood this truth when he declared in Psalm 73:28 (NIV): *"But as for me, it is good to be near God. I have made the Sovereign Lord my refuge; I will tell of all your deeds."*

Vision clarifies purpose—and through intimacy, God makes His vision clear and gives you a plan. Our God never lies; He speaks to us daily. Some time ago, I knew God had given me an assignment, but it was not clear. So, I dedicated time daily to intense worship, and gradually, the full plan was revealed to me—its location, theme, and the people I was meant to serve.

Your heart must be in alignment with God before you can clearly see the plan He has for you. For instance, if He calls you to start a community centre for disadvantaged children, your human nature might initially be filled with fear and doubt. But instead of giving in to fear, go back to God and ask Him how He wants you to carry out the assignment. I encourage you to embrace these steps as you step into your calling.

HEALTH - SPIRIT, SOUL, AND BODY

Daniel understood that the Kingdom of God goes beyond meat and drink. To fulfil his calling, his physical, spiritual, and mental health was essential for his training. He avoided heavy drinks, meat, and other indulgences. This not only kept him healthy but also gave him and his colleagues a more disciplined mind. (Daniel 1:11-15; 1 Corinthians 6:19-20; Romans 12:1; 3 John 1:2; Proverbs 4:20-22; Philippians 4:8).

As you begin your assignment, take good care of your body. It is the temple that holds your soul, and God's Spirit dwells in you. Without a healthy body, you cannot fulfil God's purpose for your life.

KNOWLEDGE FOR THE CALL

Daniel developed himself in the sciences and literature of his time. God blessed him with wisdom, giving him the ability to understand the meaning of visions and dreams. God will never call you to an area where He has not already placed the capacity in you.

For example, God may have placed you in the youth department because He knows you have a passion for abused children and a transformation spark within you whenever a child is brought to you so that you can help them find their way from darkness to light. He may also be placing it in your heart to aspire to a greater position where you can create policies that will bring change in the lives of children and future generations.

However, this transformation won't happen if you merely attend service from Monday to Friday. God wants you to have a deeper relationship with Him. The reason He wants you to show up daily is so that He can reveal strategies to you, direct you to the right books to read, guide you to the right mentors, and show you where to find funding to access the right knowledge for your calling.

LIGHT UP YOUR ALTARS

God loves your service, but He values your relationship with Him more.

To succeed in your calling, you must light up your altars by growing in intimacy with the One who called you. As you seek God daily, He will reveal all you need for the journey. He will also show you how to overcome the challenges that may arise after you answer the call.

When King Nebuchadnezzar had a troubling dream that no one could interpret, Daniel sought more time to seek the face of the Lord so he could know how to respond: *"Then Daniel returned to his house. He explained everything to his friends Hananiah, Mishael, and Azariah. He asked them to pray that the God of heaven would give him mercy. He wanted God to help him understand the mystery of the king's dream. Then he and his friends wouldn't be killed along with Babylon's other wise men. During that night, God gave Daniel a vision. He showed him what the mystery was all about. Then Daniel praised the God of heaven."* (Daniel 2:17-19, NIRV).

Because Daniel sought God's presence, he not only received the interpretation of the dream but was also elevated to a position of influence: *"Then the king appointed Daniel to a high position and gave him many valuable gifts. He made Daniel ruler over the whole province of Babylon, as well as chief over all his wise men."* (Daniel 2:48, NLT).

Now, imagine Daniel fulfilling his calling in a place full of unbelievers, yet representing God with excellence. God is calling you to do the same—to represent Him in unfamiliar territories. But you need more than a Bachelor of Science (BSc) degree to occupy that seat. You need His presence to guide you and go ahead of you.

"You will show me the path of life; In Your presence is fullness of joy; At Your right hand are pleasures forevermore." (Psalm 16:11, KJV). In God's presence, there is great manifestation. In His presence, the grace to overcome and remain steadfast in your assignment is guaranteed. And in the end, all is for His glory.

CHARACTER CHANGE

Romans 12:2 (NLT) says, *"Don't copy the behaviour and customs of this world but let God transform you into a new person by changing the way you think. Then you will learn to know God's will for you, which is good and pleasing and perfect."*

Imagine God asking you to run for mayor in your city. He is not sending you there to promote your ego, but rather, He wants you to uphold justice for the weak, be a change-maker, and make Christ-like decisions through the grace He has given you.

In fulfilling this duty, if you are ever asked to take a bribe or cover up illegal acts, remember God's Spirit is upon you to act with integrity, not as a criminal. Before sending you on such an important assignment, God would have prepared you through integrity tests. To be worthy of the assignment and succeed in it, you must possess Christ-like character.

DECLARATIONS

1. Father, Your Word says there is a time for everything. This is the time to walk in Your purpose. I receive grace for my divine assignment.

Ecclesiastes 3:1-2 (NLT): "For everything, there is a season, a time for every activity under heaven: a time to be born and a time to die, a time to plant and a time to harvest."

2. Great are Your purposes, Lord. From today, only Your purpose will prevail in my life in Jesus' name.

Proverbs 19:21 (NLT): "You can make many plans, but the Lord's purpose will prevail."

3. In the name of Jesus, I will no longer be held bound by the disappointment of yesterday. I lean on Your grace and the direction from the Holy Spirit to acquire the necessary skills for what You have called me to do. I will no longer fear or walk in shame in Jesus' name.

Isaiah 54:4 (NLT): "Fear not; you will no longer live in shame. Don't be afraid; there is no more disgrace for you."

4. Father, I decree good health for my walk with You. Sickness has been taken away from me. My soul and body are covered by the blood of Jesus.

Exodus 23:25 (KJV): "And ye shall serve the Lord your God, and he shall bless thy bread, and thy water, and I will take sickness away from the midst of thee."

5. My body is the temple of God. Therefore, I receive the wisdom to care for my body accordingly. I will feed my soul with the right nutrients.

1 Corinthians 6:19-20 (NLT): "Don't you realize that your body is the temple of the Holy Spirit, who lives in you and was given to you by God? You do not belong to yourself, for God bought you at a high price. So you must honour God with your body."

6. My heart will be merry and grateful in every season in Jesus' name. I send every stronghold of depression and confusion into the bottomless pit in Jesus' name.

Proverbs 17:22 (KJV): "A merry heart doeth good like a medicine: but a broken spirit drieth the bones."

CLOSING PRAYER

Father, I thank You for Your faithfulness and guidance. I know Your purpose for my life will prevail. Today, I receive the grace and wisdom to walk in Your calling for my life. I declare that fear, shame, and disappointment have no hold over my life.

I speak good health, peace, and joy into my life. Every stronghold of depression and confusion is destroyed in Jesus' name. Thank You for Your presence, Lord, and for guiding me through every season with victory. In Jesus' name, I pray. Amen.

CHAPTER SEVEN

WELCOME TO A NEW SEASON

"When the soul discovers its freedom, chains become powerless." - Esther Samson

ANCHOR SCRIPTURE

"It is for freedom that Christ has set us free. Stand firm, then, and do not let yourselves be burdened again by a yoke of slavery." - Galatians 5:1 (NIRV)

STEPPING INTO YOUR NEW IDENTITY

There is something deeply liberating about stepping into a new season. It marks a fresh beginning, a shift from what once held you back to the boundless possibilities ahead. Yet, stepping into something new also requires a renewed mindset—one that fully embraces freedom and refuses to return to old limitations.

You have been redeemed by the blood of Jesus. His sacrifice was the price paid to break every stronghold that once held you captive. The moment you received Jesus Christ by faith and believed in your heart that salvation was granted to you, everything changed. You became united with Him—you died with Him and rose again. This is now your new identity, your new belief system (Galatians 5:1, NIRV).

With this understanding, no power of darkness, no circumstances, and no weakness can disqualify you from walking in your new season. The only thing God requires from you is faith—to remain in Him, obey His commandments, and keep your heart open to the guidance of the Holy Spirit. *"For God has not given us a spirit of fear and timidity, but of power, love, and self-discipline."* (2 Timothy 1:7, NLT).

When you embrace this truth, you will no longer live as one bound by fear, doubt, or past failures. Instead, His glory will be evident in you and through you. You are free. Now, walk boldly in that freedom.

YOUR SEAT OF AUTHORITY AWAITS YOU

Time is short, and this is no longer about us; it is about the Kingdom of God, which is already present on earth. Jesus Christ is coming soon, and when you reach the gates of heaven, you won't be asked to present your certifications, wealth, or the possessions you have acquired. What truly matters is whether you understand why you were born and whether you are living with that understanding.

So, take the coming months, or even all of 2025, to ask God, "What do you want me to do?" I can't promise you will hear a booming voice from the heavens or a gentle whisper in your ear, but if you quiet the anxiety in your heart, still your emotions, and silence external distractions, dedicating yourself to His presence, you will find the answers you seek.

DECLARATIONS

1. Father, I declare that I am free from every chain, every stronghold, and every limitation that once held me captive. I walk boldly in the freedom that Jesus Christ has granted me. I refuse to be burdened by fear, guilt, or shame. I thank You, Lord, for

redeeming me by Your precious blood. I stand firm in the freedom You have given me, knowing that I am free indeed.

Galatians 5:1 (NLT): "So Christ has truly set us free. Now make sure that you stay free, and don't get tied up again in slavery to the law."

2. Lord, I come before You in faith, declaring that I am a new creation in You. My old self has passed away, and I am made new through Your sacrifice. I am united with You in Your death and resurrection. I let go of my past and embrace the new identity You have given me. I am no longer defined by my failures but by Your grace and power. Thank You for making me a new creation.

2 Corinthians 5:17 (NLT): "This means that anyone who belongs to Christ has become a new person. The old life is gone; a new life has begun!"

3. Heavenly Father, I thank You that no power of darkness, no circumstances, and no enemy can disqualify me from walking in my new season. I stand firm in faith, knowing that the greater One lives in me. I declare that I have been empowered by Your Holy Spirit to overcome every challenge. Fear and doubt have no place in my life. I am victorious in Christ.

2 Timothy 1:7 (NLT): "For God has not given us a spirit of fear and timidity but of power, love, and self-discipline."

4. Father, I thank You because I am victorious through the finished work of Jesus Christ. I declare that I am no longer bound by fear, doubt, or past failures. I walk in the victory You have given me. I declare that Your glory shines through me, and I will fulfil my God-given purpose. I will no longer be a slave to fear, but a child of God, walking in the freedom and victory You have provided.

Romans 8:15 (KJV): "For ye have not received the spirit of bondage again to fear; but ye have received the Spirit of adoption, whereby we cry, Abba, Father."

5. Father, I declare that I will fulfil Your purpose for my life. I receive Your grace, wisdom, and strength to walk in alignment with Your will. Empower me by Your Holy Spirit to complete every assignment You have given me. May Your glory be evident in everything I do. Let my life be a testimony of Your goodness, and may I reflect Your light in every season. Amen.

Ephesians 2:10 (KJV): "For we are His workmanship, created in Christ Jesus unto good works, which God hath before ordained that we should walk in them."

CLOSING PRAYERS

Thank You, Jesus, for washing me clean from all guilt and condemnation. Thank You for granting me the authority to overcome the flesh, the world, and the devil.

I receive Your grace and guidance to continually discover Your perfect vision for my life and to fulfil my purpose according to Your standards here on earth. May my life be a testimony that draws others closer to Jesus. Thank You for the wisdom to reflect Jesus Christ, Yahweh, and the Holy Spirit in everything I do. Amen.

FINAL REFLECTIONS
IGNITE YOUR AUTHORITY AND FULFIL YOUR GOD-GIVEN MANDATE

"Your purpose is not just a dream; it is a divine assignment waiting to be fulfilled. When you step into your calling, you step into the greatness God has already ordained for you." - Esther Samson

Dear Reader,

I celebrate you for making it to the final page of this book. Your dedication and desire to fulfil your God-given purpose are evident. But as you move forward from here, remember this: you are qualified. Everything you need to walk in your divine purpose has already been deposited within you. The question is not whether you have what it takes; the question is, are you ready to take the step?

The path to fulfilling your God-given mandate begins with action. It is time to rise above the doubts, the insecurities, and the excuses. You have the authority, the calling, and the ability to serve God and make a difference in the world. Now is the time to step out in faith!

So, start now, no matter how small. Take the lessons from this book, apply them daily, and watch how God uses you in ways beyond your imagination. Your life is meant to impact others, bring glory to God, and fulfil the purpose for which you were created.

Don't wait for perfection—God can use you where you are. As you trust Him, He will equip you, guide you, and empower you to walk boldly in your calling.

Don't hold back; the world needs your contribution, your gifts, and your voice.

Embrace your calling, walk in faith, and fulfil your God-given mandate—impacting lives and glorifying God in everything you do.

OTHER BOOKS BY THE AUTHOR

Here are other powerful books by the author that are worth reading:

- *Trials of a Woman*

- *Surviving the Storm*

- *Strategic Roles in Diplomatic Matters*

- *Dealing with Insecurities + Wise Words*

- *Love in the Northern Sahara – Book 1*

- *Journey to the Unknown – Book 2*

- *True Surrender*

- *111 Wise Thoughts*

- *105 Wise Words*

Upcoming Books:

- *The Widow's Plight*

- *To Love Again*

- *Stepmother from Hell*

These life-changing books can be purchased at the author's online bookstores through these links:

Amazon: <u>Esther Samson's Books</u>
Selar: <u>Esther Samson Ukaria</u>

HOW TO LEAVE A REVIEW

Thank you for purchasing and reading this book! The author would greatly appreciate it if you could leave a review on her Amazon and Selar bookstores. You can also connect with her and tag her on her social media pages through these links:

Facebook: Esther Samson Ukaria

Instagram: words_of_esther_samson

Linkedin: Dr.hc. Esther Samson Ukaria

Tiktok: Esther Samsom98

Website: http://www.dresthersamsonukaria.com

For invitations to book readings, speaking engagements at conferences, and workshops, kindly send an email to: estherukaria@yahoo.co.uk

AUTHOR'S INFORMATION

For questions or feedback, reach out to the author via:

Email:estherukaria@yahoo.co.uk

Facebook: Esther Samson Ukaria

Instagram: words_of_esther_samson

Linkedin: Dr. hc. Esther Samson Ukaria

Website:http://www.dresthersamsonukaria.com

Amazon Store: Esther Samson's Books

Selar Store: Esther Samson Ukaria

ABOUT THE BOOK

"Your divine assignment awaits — embrace grace, walk in authority."

Do you feel unqualified for the calling God has placed on your life? Are shame, guilt, or the approval of others holding you back? It is time to break free from these limiting beliefs and step boldly into your divine purpose!

In this powerful book, "Calling the Unqualified," the author shares personal encounters and Spirit-led insights that expose the lies keeping you stuck. Through real-life experiences, you will discover why many doubt their calling — even when they sense God's hand upon them — and how to silence those doubts with the truth: you are qualified.

You are blood-bought, adopted, and designed to shine God's light. Your struggles have not diminished you—they have refined you, preparing you for greater impact. This book will shift your focus from your limitations to God's limitless power, equipping you to walk in authority and fulfil your God-given mandate.

Now is the time to rise. You are called. You are chosen. Lives are waiting for your obedience and manifestation!

ABOUT THE AUTHOR

Esther Samson is the founder of The Lighthouse Outreach and House of Mercy Network Foundation, where she is passionate about helping individuals grow spiritually and develop personally.

She is a Christian non-fiction author who writes extensively on spiritual growth and Christian living. She is also a contemporary fiction writer, known for weaving romance and drama into her captivating stories. With a heart for teaching and mentoring, this is her 10th book.

Beyond writing, Esther works part-time as a Personal Assistant in the insurance sector. She currently lives in Mülheim, Germany.

Made in the USA
Coppell, TX
20 March 2025